JAZZ
MY MUSIC, MY PEOPLE

JAZZ

MY MUSIC, MY PEOPLE

By Morgan Monceaux

Foreword by Wynton Marsalis

Alfred A. Knopf, Publisher · New York

To my mother, Johnetta,
and my friend and mentor, Morgan Rank

THIS IS A BORZOI BOOK PUBLISHED BY ALFRED A. KNOPF, INC.

Copyright © 1994 by Morgan Monceaux and Morgan Rank Gallery
All rights reserved under International and Pan-American Copyright Conventions. Published in the United States of America by Alfred A. Knopf, Inc.,
New York, and simultaneously in Canada by Random House of Canada Limited, Toronto. Distributed by Random House, Inc., New York.
Manufactured in Singapore   10 9 8 7 6 5 4 3 2
Library of Congress Cataloging-in-Publication Data
Monceaux, Morgan. Jazz: my music, my people / written and illustrated by Morgan Monceaux. p.   cm.   ISBN 0-679-85618-8 (trade)
1. Jazz musicians – United States – Biography.   I. Title. ML3929.M65   1994   781.65′092′2 – dc20   [B] 93-38177
Designed by Eileen Rosenthal

The paintings in this book were done on Archer paper, using pastels, paint, Pentel markers, and multimedia collage.

CONTENTS

INTRODUCTION

This book got its start in our living room during the 1950s as my sister and I listened to my mother, a blues singer, rehearse material for her club performances. When I was a child, I didn't think of jazz as a separate body of music. It was just what we listened to every day growing up in Louisiana.

In my family, everyone sang. I didn't take singing lessons from a music teacher—I had my mother. Her grandfather was a minister, and we all sang for him in church: my mother, my grandmother, my great-grandmother, my sister, me. Whenever it was required, we sang for him.

We sang for ourselves, too, and played the piano. And that's how every musician I've included in this book started out—singing or playing an instrument for themselves and for those around them. They were young, often still in their teens, when they started making a living as musicians. In the early years of jazz, they were almost never formally trained. They were professional musicians in the days when no African American, no matter how accomplished, could play in a symphony orchestra.

The musicians in this book are the great rule-breakers of our time. Like all musicians, they listened to the music around them and learned to play what they heard. And then they created new sounds—a distinct American and an African-American music that had never been heard before. Jazz is an oral tradition—it's like storytelling. One person hears something and passes it on. Buddy Bolden influenced a generation of New Orleans brassmen, including Louis Armstrong, who influenced Dizzy Gillespie, who influenced Miles Davis. Lester Young's saxophone influenced Charlie Parker, who influenced John Coltrane, who continues to influence many others. As one performer listens to another, bringing personal experience to their improvised sounds, a music evolves. We can hear it in recordings that nearly, but not quite, span the lifetime of jazz. We can hear it in the songs of Bessie Smith and Billie Holiday and the singers who followed, as they learned to use their voices like a musical instrument. We can hear the instrumentalists emulating the singers in turn.

As we grew up, my sister and I were encouraged to make something of ourselves, to find role models who were black, people we could look up to and be proud of. Someone like Nat King Cole meant the world to my family, because he was the first African American to have his own television show—the *first*. My grandparents wanted us to be able to say, "I have ability and talent. I have something to offer the world, and I'm good at what I do."

Music has been part of every day of my life, and during the hard times, it helped me hold my sanity. With this book, I wanted to put my emotional response to music into paintings. And I wanted to tell the stories of the performers who brought their own experiences and emotions as Americans and African Americans to their concerts and jam sessions and recordings. But if you have never listened to the music, my paintings can't tell you everything. After you read this book, put it down and listen...to Leadbelly, Bessie Smith, Miles Davis, Louis Armstrong. They have their own stories to tell. You can hear it in the music.

Morgan Monceaux
New York City

FOREWORD: THE LEGEND OF BUDDY BOLDEN

They say that in order to know the real meaning of a thing you must go back to the beginning. In the beginning you will find the end, and from those two points you can divine everything in between. That is why it is very important for us to know the name of a New Orleans man—Buddy Bolden. More than being the first jazz musician, Buddy Bolden is a heroic symbol of jazz music itself.

All kinds of people liked Kid Bolden. He knew how to listen. Not just to what he wanted to hear—but to the actual meaning of what was being told. Something in the eyes and face of the boy made people reveal themselves. Maybe it was his vitality, or humor, or intelligence, but it was probably his understanding. You see, Buddy wasn't too big on talking. He would use that talking energy to concentrate on people's expressed desires. People were always asking him for advice, ideas, or just plain old opinion. Since Buddy loved making people feel good, when he did talk, he would oblige them. He told the men what the ladies liked, the chumps what the hustlers were like, the sinners how they were like the saved, and where the best food, drink, and times were to be had. His was the voice of wisdom—an active combination of accuracy, interest, and good intention.

On weekdays, Buddy cut hair and shaved faces at Mr. Cherry's barbershop. He would stand all day under that big, slow-moving wooden fan, razor in hand, listening and talking the hottest information and gossip known to woman and man. At other times, Buddy Bolden could be found at picnics, socials, and parades, his trumpet in hand, wielded with the same precision and style as his noonday razor, intently swinging to shave the dusty excesses out of people's hearts and minds. The Buddy everyone loved was at the helm of a band of local working men armed with tuba, trombone, clarinet, drum, banjo—and equally intent on rocking the demons of everyday living into unremitting slumber. They liked to play blues so everyone could *hear* what was what, even the church sisters (though they wouldn't admit it). They liked to play jazz so everyone could *know* what was what. Yes! Everyone loved their Buddy uncut. And what came steaming out of his horn on these occasions was the very hottest gossip—an intensity of relationships so volatile that you could embarrass yourselves thinking and feeling 'em. When King Bolden raised his horn and blew, Gabriel's cheeks flushed hot with the panic of insecurity. So confidently did Bolden's sound shout out against the gumbo-thick New Orleans sky that people way across the Mississippi River in Algiers could clearly hear that it was time to swing with a happiness that infected all within earshot.

The music was so old that it was new every time you heard it. It went so far back that time just looped around to today. Buddy Bolden's music was syncopated; so they all danced. It was the blues; so they all danced with feeling. It was jazz; so they all danced with feeling and accuracy. And it swung; so they all danced *together* with feeling and accuracy. Too much of a good thing. Too much of a good thing! Buddy Bolden played so much horn that he blew his mind through the bell of a trumpet and left his soul to carry on. And carry on it did, in the souls and horns and voices of all those who play jazz music—Buddy Bolden's children.

Wynton Marsalis
New York City

BUDDY BOLDEN

Trumpeter, bandleader

1868-1931

I first heard of Buddy Bolden when I was eleven. My papa and I were in New Orleans for a funeral, and he took me on a tour of the city. We stopped at Congo Square, where the black people of New Orleans used to come one day a week to be free. There they were able to sing and dance and practice the religious beliefs that were brought here from the old country. My father told me that jazz had begun in Congo Square and that Buddy Bolden had been the first musician to play it.

Buddy Bolden was born in 1868 in New Orleans. He was a barber by trade and had a reputation as a ladies' man. He never learned to read music, yet he taught himself to play the accordion and then the trumpet. Sometime in the 1890s, he organized a brass band.

What made it a jazz band? Bolden's musicians heard the blues, French dances, popular songs, and vodun music, with its West African drumbeats. In New Orleans, music was everywhere, and styles began to cross and blend as people like Bolden began to make new sounds out of the sounds they heard. It's impossible to know exactly what Bolden sounded like, because he never made a recording, but his band probably played with a strong, syncopated beat, like the ragtime that had become popular piano music. Some people said that Bolden played the most powerful trumpet of all time. His band played at funerals and dances and picnics, and with the opening of the Storyville red-light district in 1897, the new music found a place in the nightclubs. Bolden's career was tragically cut short in 1907, when he was committed to a mental institution. But he lived in the memories of those who had heard his trumpet and band and who played his music.

W.C. HANDY

Composer, bandleader, cornetist

1873-1958

In 1964, I was a freshman at Bishop College in Dallas, Texas. I'd heard my mother sing "Joe Turner Blues," and I decided to sing it for the music-department talent show. After the performance, I saw a girl standing in the auditorium, crying. She had felt the grief in the music, the emotion you hear when the blues are sung.

Like Buddy Bolden, W. C. Handy was a horn player and bandleader. Unlike Bolden, he could read music and had been schooled in classical music. As a young man, he played in a number of musical groups, eventually becoming the leader of the Mahara Minstrels.

W. C. Handy saw the appeal of the blues—the songs of the roadside guitar pickers and small bands that captured the everyday sorrow and heartache of life among Southern black people. The blues could be funny as well as sad, and told stories that varied each time they were sung. They were rarely written down, but Handy had the musical skills to collect and arrange them, and he began to publish them as sheet music. His first published song was "Memphis Blues," a campaign song he wrote in 1909 for Boss Crump, who was running for mayor of Memphis.

W. C. Handy has been called the "Father of the Blues," and it's because of him that this music reached a wide audience. "St. Louis Blues," "Yellow Dog Blues," "Joe Turner Blues," and "Beale Street Blues" have been performed countless times by singers and jazz ensembles. The musical features of blues—sad-sounding blue notes and brief, three-line compositions in twelve-measure form that invited improvisation—entered the language of all popular music, including jazz.

LEADBELLY

Singer, guitarist, songwriter

1885 - 1949

I always think of my grandfather and great-uncle Amos as classic black Southerners. They were strong and big, with heavy callused hands, and they worked very hard all of their lives. They were great lovers of Leadbelly and would play his records every time they got together. They would sit under the acorn trees in the backyard and laugh and smoke and sing along. The music was sad, but it was also soothing, and this listening and relaxing to Leadbelly's music went on through most of my childhood.

Leadbelly has become a legendary figure in American music. He was born Huddie Ledbetter in Mooringsport, Louisiana, and was raised in Texas. Leadbelly learned blues, folk songs, and work songs as he traveled the South as a young man, working as a farm hand and musician. In 1918, he inadvertently killed a man in a bar fight and was jailed for murder. Seven years later he was pardoned, but he was jailed again in 1930 for murderous assault. He was pardoned for the second time in 1934, after the governor of Louisiana heard him sing.

Leadbelly sang the country blues, songs of working people in the South. He knew the music of the field hands and the chain gang leaders. Accompanying himself on his twelve-string guitar, he sang of boll weevils, trains, armies, drinking, women, and life and death. Leadbelly wasn't a jazz singer, but his traditional music draws on the rhythms of western Africa and the music sung by the slaves—musical ideas that jazz performers have returned to again and again.

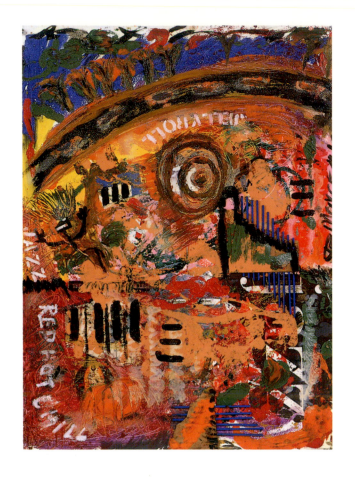

JELLY ROLL MORTON

Pianist, composer

1885-1941

Jelly Roll Morton's family attended the opera, and he claimed to have spoken only French as a child. When his grandmother learned he was playing the piano in a brothel, she made him leave home. He was a pool hall hustler, gambler, pimp – and a serious composer. He said he was the first person to use the word *jazz*, back in 1902.

He was born Ferdinand La Menthe in New Orleans. His family were Creoles, light-skinned blacks who were partly of French ancestry. He was brought up to look down on those with darker skins and continued to do so all his life. As a child, he followed the brass bands on the streets. And in the sporting houses, honky-tonks, and dance halls of Storyville, he honed his skills as a musician.

At first, Jelly Roll would have been playing ragtime, music that swept the country at the turn of the century. Its strong, syncopated rhythm was just right for dancing. But the ragtime craze didn't last, and Jelly Roll, improvising nightly, was soon adding other things to his music. From his Creole background, he knew French dances, and he'd learned Spanish rhythms like the tango. From the darker-skinned blacks who lived in New Orleans, he'd heard the blues. He'd heard the rhythms in Buddy Bolden's band. All these elements appear in his compositions, whether for piano or for bands like his Red Hot Peppers.

Jelly Roll Morton was an inventive composer, but he didn't create jazz by himself. He did treat jazz as serious music, though. He was left behind when soloists like Louis Armstrong took jazz in a new direction, but his compositions remain carefully crafted, balanced works, among the most sophisticated of their day.

14

Danny has plaled with Cab Calloway, Jell Roll Martin & Sidney Bechet... The New Orleans Jazz Museum Award Brass Band & farview Baptist Church Band Banjo Player in New Orleans Danny Barker

THE RHYTHM SECTION

Danny Barker, banjo player,

guitarist, 1908-

Louis Barbarin, drummer, 1902-

Danny Barker grew up with the brass bands of old New Orleans, and his career has lasted into the 1990s. Like his uncles, the drummers Louis and Paul Barbarin, he learned to play the banjo, which was used as a rhythm instrument in early jazz.

Most rhythm players in the first jazz bands weren't featured as soloists. Except for the pianists, they usually weren't bandleaders, and their names aren't found in the history books. But the rhythm section is the foundation of jazz. It's sometimes hard to hear it behind the wind instruments, but it's always there. In early jazz, the rhythm instruments keep the steady, even beat that allows other instruments to improvise, and the banjo might also play the basic chords that harmonize the melody. Other sounds can sometimes be heard on early recordings: a banjo strum after the main beat or the clapping of wooden blocks in a syncopated pattern. These echo the rhythmical music that Africans brought to this country: performances in which several drummers keep complex, intermingled patterns of beats, no two the same. In simplified form, these rhythms are the essence of jazz.

Since his early days in New Orleans, Danny Barker has played with Jelly Roll Morton, Cab Calloway, Sidney Bechet, and many other musicians. Louis Barbarin's career started with the Onward Brass Band in 1918, and he played professionally into the 1980s. In 1993, he received a living history award from the William Ransome Hogan Jazz Archive in New Orleans.

SIDNEY BECHET

Clarinetist, soprano saxophonist

1897-1959

Music was the only life for Sidney Bechet, who taught himself to play his brother's clarinet when he was just six years old. His grandfather was a slave; Sidney's father, also a musician, often told him about Emancipation Day, which had taken place when the elder Bechet was eight.

Sidney moved to New York City as a young man, opening his own Harlem nightclub in 1924. He also switched to soprano saxophone, which is shaped like a clarinet but has a deeper tone. Until John Coltrane took up the soprano sax in the 1950s, Bechet was almost the only jazz musician to play this instrument. And over the years, he played with almost every major big band of his day. Sidney Bechet chose to spend much of his time touring in Europe, where jazz was more popular than in the United States. For this reason, he wasn't as well known in this country as Duke Ellington or Louis Armstrong. But within the field, few instrumentalists were more respected by musicians from every jazz era.

M A RAINEY

Singer, songwriter

1886-1939

In the early years of the twentieth century, blacks moved north in great numbers. They found homes and jobs in the big northern cities. But they were often homesick for their families in the South, and for the blues, the music they'd heard back home. In the 1920s, record companies discovered there was a market for the blues. Ma Rainey was one of the first true blues stars.

Ma Rainey was born Gertrude Pridgett to a family of traveling minstrels and was trained as a singer and entertainer. In her early teens, she married another performer. For years she and her husband traveled, performing at circuses and vaudeville and minstrel shows. She stayed in the South nearly all her life, although recording sessions occasionally brought her north. By the time she became a blues star, she was close to forty. A large woman, she loved fancy clothes and flashy jewelry. She had a raw, powerful, gutsy voice. She wrote many of her songs and sang them with equal parts sadness and humor.

BESSIE SMITH

Singer

1894-1937

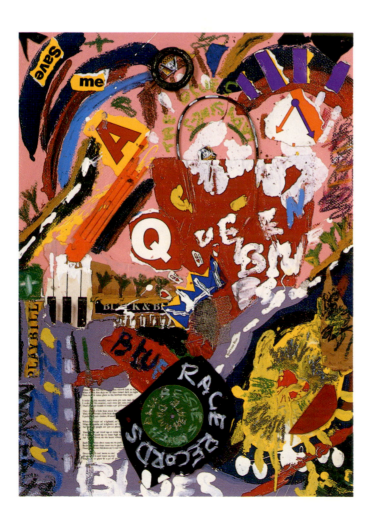

When I moved to New York in 1990, I could not find steady work. For a time I took shelter in an abandoned building in the Bronx. While eating tuna out of the can, I listened to tapes of Bessie Smith. Her songs gave me the strength to see tomorrow.

If Ma Rainey was the first great blues singer, her protégée, Bessie Smith, became the first great jazz singer. Born in Tennessee and discovered at the age of thirteen by Ma Rainey, she toured the South for years with Rainey's Rabbit Foot Minstrels.

Bessie Smith made her first recording in 1923. It sold 800,000 copies, and by 1925 she was the highest-paid musician in jazz. Her records, like those of many early jazz performers, were released on what were commonly called race labels, distributed almost exclusively to blacks. She had a powerful voice that stood up unusually well to early recording techniques. But by 1930 her career had faltered under the weight of alcoholism and other problems, and she died several years later in an automobile accident.

When she was on stage, Bessie Smith had the charisma of an evangelist—she was a true performer. And as a musician, she knew exactly what she wanted to do. Using her voice like an instrument, she could slide up and down a pitch, dramatically varying her timing and intonation, getting all the emotion of everyday speech into her singing. Known by her fans as the "Empress of the Blues," Bessie Smith was always a blues singer, but with accompanists like Louis Armstrong, she showed that she could swing.

1

2

WOMEN SINGERS OF THE 1920s

1. Josephine Baker, 1906 - 1975; 2. Mamie Smith, 1883 - 1946

3. Ethel Waters, 1896 - 1977; 4. Olivia Charlot, 1913 -

If life was hard for the men who made their living playing jazz, it demanded even more from the women, especially if they went on the road. It took stamina and courage to endure the loneliness and survive in a man's world. Nonetheless, some of the women who sang in the early years of jazz were among the most popular artists of their day.

Josephine Baker, while not a true jazz or blues singer, brought the idea of jazz to Paris, where she became a great star. Mamie Smith got her start as a vaudeville singer, and in 1920 recorded "Crazy Blues," the first big blues hit. Ethel Waters, who was often known by the nickname "Sweet Mama Stringbean," took jazz and blues singing from the nightclubs to the big screen, becoming one of the highest-paid black performers in Hollywood. And Olivia Charlot was a singer, pianist, and organist who brought New Orleans–style jazz into the 1930s and beyond.

Louis Armstrong

Trumpeter, singer, bandleader, composer, 1900-1971

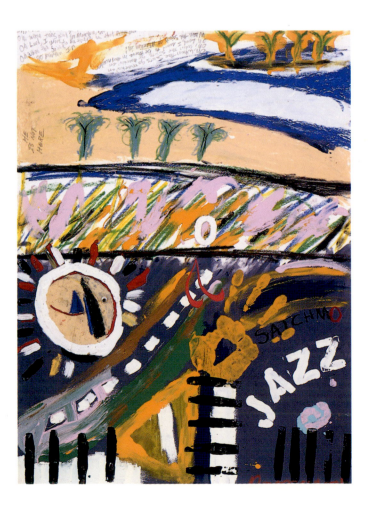

When I was just ten years old, my great-uncle Amos died. Uncle Amos was an amateur musician, and Louis Armstrong was his friend. Louis and the great gospel singer Mahalia Jackson came to Fordoche, Louisiana, to sing at his funeral. It was a traditional New Orleans funeral. Mahalia stood in the back of a truck and sang from the church to the cemetery. Louis played from the church to the cemetery and then back to the church and to our house. I have never seen or heard anything like it, and it has stayed with me all my life.

Louis was born in New Orleans, and his parents separated soon after his birth. At the age of twelve, he fired a pistol into the air and was sent to a reform school, where he learned to play the cornet. When he was released, he supported himself and his mother by delivering coal and began to work as a musician.

He moved to Chicago in 1922, recording with Bessie Smith and playing in the big bands of King Oliver and Fletcher Henderson. Later, with his own bands, he gained international fame for his warm, pure trumpet tone, his improvisational skill, and his quick, gravelly voice. Nicknamed "Satchmo," Armstrong became known for "scat," wordless singing in which the voice imitates a musical instrument. He was the first to record it.

Louis Armstrong changed the sound of jazz. More than any other musician, he crossed African and New Orleans rhythms with European harmonies, creating the infectious dance rhythms of swing music. Early New Orleans jazz bands had a collective sound: while the trumpet predominated, each instrument played a separate melody and rhythm that complemented the others. With Armstrong, jazz became an art based on soloists within an ensemble. This idea, together with his ideas of phrasing and rhythm, has influenced musicians since the 1920s.

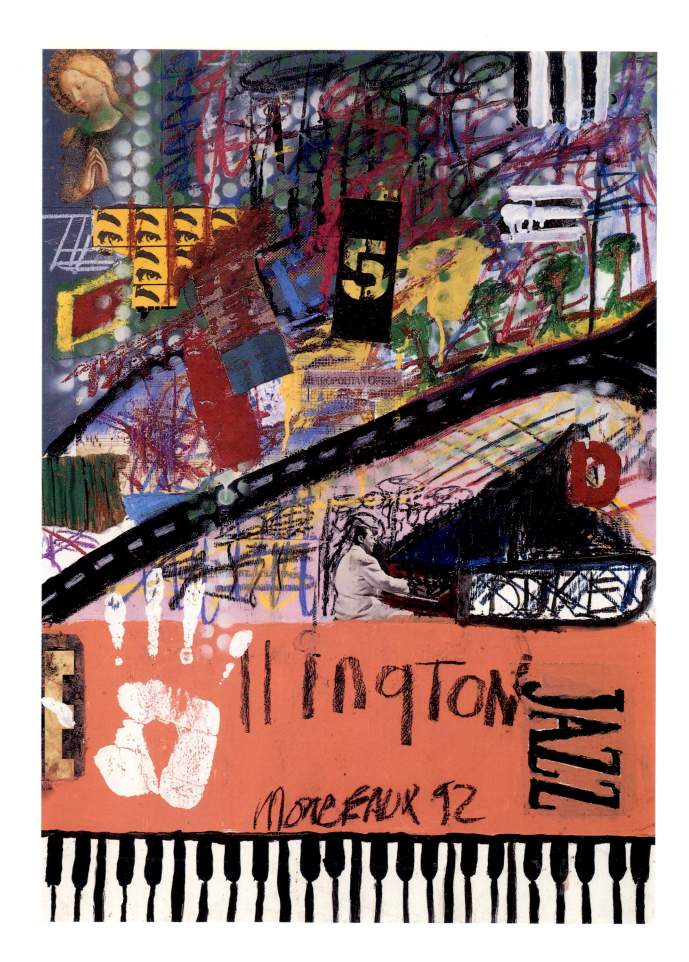

In 1955, my aunt graduated from Grambling College. The commencement ceremony opened with Duke Ellington's "In the Beginning," one of his sacred compositions. Its tone suited the occasion exactly and opened my mind to the many faces of his music.

Ellington has been called the greatest of all jazz composers, but he didn't hear jazz or blues when he was growing up. Born in Washington, D.C., he took piano lessons as a child and taught himself to play ragtime. His first bands played popular songs, but after moving to New York City, he heard New Orleans music and started playing jazz. In 1927, his band was engaged to play at the Cotton Club, a Harlem nightclub that catered to white audiences. Over the next few years, he learned to compose, as his band backed the club's elaborate floor show. Gradually, he began to put the spirit and the sounds of Harlem – the center of black cultural life at the time – into his music.

Another musician once said, "Ellington plays the piano, but his real instrument is his band." Ellington wrote for the musicians who played for him, and encouraged them to develop their own sounds. Growling, muted brass instruments, liquid clarinets, and smooth saxophones all had a place in his band, and were blended together with skill and subtlety. He used his piano to drive the rhythm of the piece and provide harmonies. His compositions vary from the raucous jungle beat of his Cotton Club days to the smooth dance music of the swing era to haunting, impressionistic mood pieces.

Ellington's works have a sound that is unmistakable, and he never forgot that jazz is dance music. His music not only encompassed his era but went beyond it, and he is considered one of the greatest composers – of any form of music – of the twentieth century.

DUKE ELLINGTON

Pianist, bandleader, composer

1899 - 1974

COUNT BASIE

Pianist, bandleader, composer

1904 - 1984

When I was eleven years old, my mother and grandmother arranged a surprise anniversary party for my great-grandparents. It was held at the Starlight Ballroom in Chicago, where Count Basie was performing. To this day, I remember Count Basie on the bandstand and my great-grandparents dancing to that beautiful music.

Count Basie was born in New Jersey, but his first job in music was in Kansas City, a city with a large population of musicians and jazz clubs. He worked there for a year as a pianist in a silent-movie theater and played in the bands of Walter Page and Bennie Moten. He formed his own group in 1935 and a year later moved to New York City.

For people like my parents and grandparents, Count Basie *was* the swing era. In the 1930s and early 1940s, the big bands were broadcast nightly on radio stations across the country, and jazz found a wider audience than ever before. Basie's band, like many of the others, was large, with as many as seventeen men. The rhythm section was at the heart of it: Basie's clean, spare piano, with outstanding players on guitar, string bass, and drums. While players soloed in turn, the rest of the saxophones and brass would play riffs—brief snatches of melody played over and over, swinging above the beat. As one chorus followed another, the riffs built in intensity and drama. It was the perfect music to dance to, spirited and powerful.

Basie's band has survived in one form or another for over fifty years. In 1957, it was the first American jazz band to play for the Queen of England, a fitting occasion for a man called Count.

CAB CALLOWAY

Singer, bandleader, composer

1907 -

My great-grandmother was a very religious woman, but she was fun-loving, too. She liked to dance and she *loved* Cab Calloway. When she cleaned house, she'd put on his record, "Minnie the Moocher." Then she'd dance with her duster, singing "hi de hi de ho" along with Cab.

Cab Calloway led one of the most popular jazz orchestras of the swing era, and he found success at a very young age. By the time he was twenty-two, he was already being booked into the Cotton Club, filling in for the Ellington band. From the first, he had an instinct for entertainment as well as music. Minnie the Moocher was one of a number of characters created by Calloway in songs set in and around Harlem. Working scat and jive talk into his vocals, Calloway created a singing style all his own. Backed by top-notch musicians, he sang tenor, baritone, and bass, and is considered the most gifted male singer of the early swing era.

With his band and alone, Cab Calloway performed in many movies, from *Stormy Weather* in 1943 to *The Blues Brothers* in 1980. And in 1952, he played the role of the fast-talking, sharply dressed Sportin' Life in a Broadway production of *Porgy and Bess,* a part George Gershwin wrote with Calloway in mind.

JIMMY RUSHING

Singer

1903 - 1972

Male singers were scarce in the early days of jazz. Jimmy Rushing was an exception. Known as "Mr. Five-by-Five" because of his size, Rushing sang with Count Basie's band from 1935 to 1950.

Jimmy Rushing came from a family of musicians; his father played the trumpet, and his mother and brother were pianists. Rushing himself played the violin and piano as a child, and sang with his church choir. He left home in his teens and drifted, working pick-up jobs as a musician. One of his first professional engagements was with Jelly Roll Morton in California. Starting in 1928, he toured with Walter Page's Blue Devils and later with Bennie Moten's band, where he met many of the musicians who would form Count Basie's band.

Like many of the big band musicians who worked in Kansas City in the 1930s, Rushing had a background in the blues. He was the best known of the blues shouters, and his high-pitched, penetrating voice could sometimes be heard ten blocks away, ringing above Basie's large swing band. But Rushing's style, like that of Bessie Smith, crossed from blues to jazz. Where a blues singer would sing on the beat, Rushing sometimes anticipated it, swinging as hard as any musician in the band.

LESTER YOUNG

Tenor saxophonist

1909 - 1959

Billie Holiday gave him his nickname back when both of them were in the Basie band and Lester was living with Billie and her mother in Harlem. Lester was the greatest, she figured, as good as President Roosevelt. After that, "Pres" was what all the musicians called him.

In the earliest jazz bands, the cornet and clarinet had the big solo roles. But by the 1930s, the saxophone had become increasingly important. And Lester Young, one of the great and controversial tragic figures in jazz, was first among the saxophonists of his day.

Lester Young's father was a carnival musician, and Lester traveled with him through the South and Midwest. He started as a drummer but switched to saxophone as a teenager, because he found that by the time he had packed up the drums after a performance, all the girls had left. He ran away from home at the age of eighteen and traveled during the next few years with different bands. Eventually, he landed a job in Kansas City with the Basie band.

At first, people made fun of Pres's sound; it was thin, they said, not robust enough for the big bands. But other musicians came to appreciate his gifts, and soon nearly everyone who came to Kansas City wanted to take him on in a cutting contest. A master improviser, he could play a melody like no one else, and his solos sounded almost like speech – or a song. He chose harmonies that were simpler than those played by other soloists of the swing era, pointing the way for some of the innovations that would soon change jazz completely. But Lester Young was drafted into the army in 1944, and the war changed him. He got caught up in drugs and became a heroin addict. His career started going downhill. He spent the rest of his life in Europe, performing in small clubs, and never entirely broke free of his addiction.

ART TATUM

Pianist

1910 - 1956

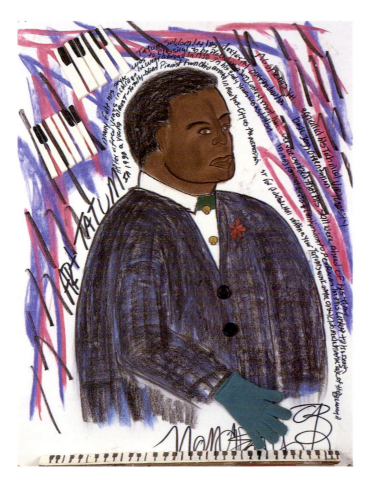

My grandfather taught my sister to play the piano. At the end of each lesson, he'd play a record by Art Tatum and tell her to repeat the sounds she had just heard. She would sit at the piano, practicing a phrase over and over, never getting it exactly right, but never giving up.

In 1932, a young, nearly blind pianist from Ohio arrived in New York City. Art Tatum had been born with cataracts in both eyes. His mother recognized his musical talent when he was three. She knew that if this gift was developed, he'd have a way to earn a living. He started piano lessons as a young child, learning to read musical notation in Braille. Originally trained in classical music, Tatum was drawn to jazz by the radio broadcasts he heard. Within a year of his arrival in New York, talk of his unbeatable performance in the cutting contests electrified the jazz world. Dating from jazz's earliest days, these contests let musicians test their skill against one another, sometimes for an audition in a band. Tatum could outplay anyone at the piano. He could play by ear anything he heard, at tempos few musicians could match. His recordings show dazzling runs of speed and imaginative harmonies, with a technical mastery unmatched in the history of jazz. His rhythm was subtle and sure, an individual's expression of the swing era.

Unlike most performers of his time, Tatum nearly always worked as a soloist or with a trio. At the time of his death, he had won the respect reserved for those who totally dominate their art.

MARY LOU WILLIAMS

Pianist, composer, arranger

1910-1981

Boogie-woogie that's straight from the honky-tonks… smooth big-band arrangements… sacred music… bebop. They're all a part of the work of Mary Lou Williams. A true child prodigy, she started at the age of six playing at parties in Pittsburgh, where she grew up. In her early teens, she left home to join the vaudeville circuit, playing at circuses and minstrel shows to help support her family. Eventually she found work with the big bands, playing the piano and writing the arrangements for their numbers. Working with the bands, alone, or with her own trio, she had one of the most varied careers in jazz.

As a pianist, Williams was versatile, incorporating diverse styles into her improvisation. She was open to innovation and worked with the bebop pioneers on the unusual harmonies that she at first called "zombie music," because they sounded so strange. Persistent as well as talented, she was virtually the only woman to make a living solely as an instrumentalist during the first decades of jazz.

BILLIE HOLIDAY

Singer

1915-1959

36

I found Billie Holiday in my second year of high school. One day I was walking down the road to the general store when a group of white men drove past me in a car and called me a nigger. I went home in tears. When I told my grandmother what had happened, she played Billie's record of "Strange Fruit," a song about a lynching. From that day on, it was love.

She led a hard life. Her parents were unmarried teenagers: a maid and a traveling musician. She was raped by a neighbor at age ten; he went to jail, and she was sent to a home for wayward girls. Later, she and her mother moved to Harlem, where Billie, at fifteen, worked in a brothel. Then she auditioned for a dancer's job in a nightclub. She gave such a bad performance that the pianist asked if she could sing. And sing she could. She reduced the audience to tears and was hired on the spot.

No one sang like Billie Holiday. Her voice was beautiful, dark as night. She didn't have the gutsiness of Ma Rainey or Bessie Smith. But like Bessie Smith, whose music she'd heard as a child, Billie Holiday poured her feelings into every-thing she sang. Her other inspiration was Louis Armstrong, and her phrasing, sense of swing, and way of improvising upon the written melody drew on his style. She wasn't a blues singer, but she often "bent" notes—distorting them in blues fash-ion. She was at her best with gifted musicians like Lester Young, who would improvise behind her, weaving through her song so her voice seemed to be another instrument in the band. She wrote, "I hate straight singing. I have to change a tune to my own way of doing it. That's all I know."

Addicted to heroin for most of her adult life, Billie Holiday lived fast and always close to the edge. But her legacy is in the hundreds of songs that she recorded with musical artistry and emo-tional truth.

My cousin Stella lived next door to us in the 1950s. She'd sit on her porch after dinner, smoking cigars. When she wanted my sister and me to come in for the evening, she'd play an Ella Fitzgerald record. I got my first lessons in scat singing on those nights, out on the porch with my sister and cousin, listening to Ella.

Like Billie Holiday, Ella Fitzgerald got her start at a young age. Orphaned at the age of fifteen, she was living in an orphanage and making the rounds of amateur talent contests in Harlem when she was discovered two years later. A saxophonist in Chick Webb's big band heard her and made her promise to audition with Webb. But Webb wasn't excited about having a singer in his band. When he heard Ella, though, he changed his mind.

While singing with Chick Webb's band, Ella Fitzgerald became a star. In the years since, she has sung with Duke Ellington, Count Basie, Louis Armstrong, and many others. Her audience reaches beyond fans of jazz: many people know her for her albums of show music and popular songs. As a pop singer, her voice is warm and perfectly suited for ballads. As a jazz singer, she is best known for scat singing. She is a gifted improviser and interpreter, swinging with rhythmic subtlety and suiting her vocal style to that of the band.

Ella Fitzgerald is an ambassador; like Louis Armstrong, she's one of the few musicians who have reached a wide audience that might not otherwise listen to jazz. No other jazz vocalist is as well known and acclaimed as she.

ELLA FITZGERALD

Singer

1918 -

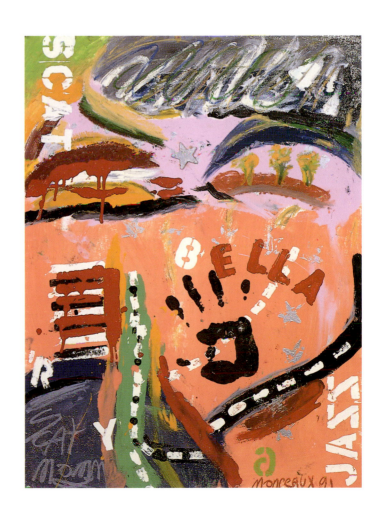

1   2

THE LADIES WHO SWING THE BAND

1. Ivie Anderson, 1904 - 1949; 2. Dorothy Dandridge, 1923 - 1965

3. The International Sweethearts of Rhythm, 1935 - 1948

4. Nina Mae McKinney, 1909 - 1967

5. Sister Rosetta Tharpe, 1921 - 1973

In the swing era, bandleaders became aware that a woman singer who was young and pretty could increase their popularity, although the musicians themselves usually weren't enthusiastic about giving a singer lead billing. The women singers often had a hard time winning the respect of serious musicians, but sometimes they went on to become stars.

Ivie Anderson sang with the Ellington band for eleven years. Her strong voice meshed well with the Ellington saxophones and brass. Dorothy Dandridge was a singer with Count Basie's band who went on to become a movie actress. Her first film was the Marx Brothers' *A Day at the Races,* and she later starred in a movie version of *Porgy and Bess.* Nina Mae McKinney was a jazz diva who sang with Count Basie's band as well as with Eubie Blake and his orchestra in the 1932 black short film *Pie Pie Blackbird.* The International Sweethearts of Rhythm was the most famous and hottest women's jazz band in the 1940s as well as one of the first racially integrated jazz ensembles. Sister Rosetta Tharpe was a gospel singer who brought religious music into a secular setting, starting with a 1938 engagement with Cab Calloway at the Cotton Club.

3

4

5

CHARLIE PARKER

Alto saxophonist, composer, bandleader, 1920 -1955

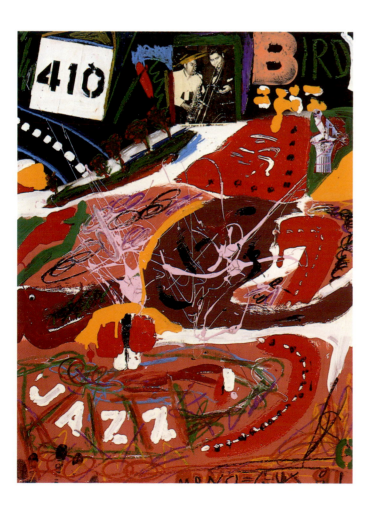

When my mother was away on one of her singing trips, the house would seem too quiet. Then she'd come home and have all her friends over for a party. They'd bring the new records they'd bought while she was away, and the house would be filled with people swaying and popping their fingers and dancing. It was at one of these parties that I first heard Charlie Parker.

Charlie Parker's mother raised him alone in Kansas City. In the same year that Count Basie was starting his own band, Parker was in high school, teaching himself to play the saxophone. At fifteen, still too young to go into nightclubs, he'd spend his evenings outside them, listening. When he started jamming with professional musicians, he was often laughed off the band-stand. He kept playing, though. At eighteen, he moved to Chicago and then New York City, work-ing for a time as a dishwasher in a restaurant where Art Tatum had a gig. Slowly, he began to get work as a musician.

Parker was playing in swing bands, but he was hearing different sounds in his head. In after-hours jam sessions at small clubs, he and other young musicians were working on a new kind of music. Not everyone liked this new jazz; it was too fast to dance to, with accents and phrasing that changed the rhythms completely. And the notes didn't sound right—they were from the parts of chords that people weren't used to hearing. But Charlie Parker was playing better than almost anyone else. When he played the new music, other musicians listened.

Charlie Parker, nicknamed "Bird," became famous for his saxophone playing, but his per-sonal problems began to interfere with his music. He was addicted to drugs and alcohol, and led a fast life that aged him quickly. He was only thirty-four when he died. He was a revolutionary, and he sent jazz in a new direction.

DIZZY GILLESPIE

Trumpeter, composer, bandleader

1917-1992

He was nicknamed "Dizzy" because he was always clowning around. But some people said he was dizzy like a fox, and as smart as they come. John Birks Gillespie grew up in South Carolina, the youngest of nine children in a musical family. Dizzy showed his musical gift early and studied trombone, trumpet, and music theory in school. When his mother moved to Philadelphia after his father's death, Dizzy went with her. There, while still a teenager, he began playing in local swing bands. In 1939, he got a job with Cab Calloway's band.

Like Charlie Parker, Dizzy Gillespie was experimenting with new ways of playing jazz. Big-band music was still popular, but some of the younger musicians were finding it too predictable. Gillespie's solos had started to sound strange, at least to Cab Calloway himself, who fired him, ostensibly for throwing a spitball. And the new music – called bebop – was harder to master than swing, with dissonant chords and a fast beat with eccentric rhythms that weren't easy to dance to. A labor dispute between musicians and the record companies led to a union ban on recordings during the early 1940s, when bebop first developed. But by the time the ban was lifted in 1944, Gillespie had emerged as a leader in getting the music accepted by other musicians and the general public.

The bell on Dizzy Gillespie's trumpet soared upward, originally the result of an accident; but he kept it that way so he could more easily hear himself and other musicians. His sound was clear and powerful, looking to drum licks and Afro-Cuban rhythms for inspiration. The teenaged clown who couldn't sit still on the bandstand had become a respected performer, playing authentic bebop into the 1990s.

THELONIOUS MONK

Pianist, composer

1917-1982

In my junior year of high school, my father's younger brother, Huey Lee, came to live in our town. I remember him playing Thelonious Monk's records for my father. "You have to hear this," he'd say. "This guy Monk is crazy." The piano we heard sounded electric. The music seemed to run from one corner of the room to the other, and it made the hair on my head stand on end.

Thelonious Monk was exactly Dizzy Gillespie's age. He grew up in New York City, and like so many jazz musicians, he began playing professionally in his teens. Monk found an after-hours home at Minton's, a Harlem nightclub that was a favorite hangout for Parker, Gillespie, and other young bebop players. So many musicians showed up wanting to play at jam sessions that Monk and Gillespie started working out increasingly complex arrangements for the sessions, hoping to scare away the less talented. Monk once said, "We're going to create something that they can't steal because they can't play it." And their new music grew more sophisticated as a result.

Both Monk and Art Tatum preferred to play the piano alone or in small groups. But their styles couldn't have been more different. Where Tatum would fill every musical space with sound, Monk was a minimalist. He played at slower tempos than Parker and Gillespie, and his phrasing and harmonies — the way his notes fitted into chords — seemed even more unusual than those of the horn players. Monk was a composer as well, and several of his pieces, like "'Round Midnight" and "Ruby, My Dear," have become standards. Monk is one of the true originals in jazz, influencing musicians well beyond the bebop period.

NAT KING COLE

Singer, pianist

1916 -1965

In 1980, my mother and I drove from Louisiana to San Francisco with her Yorkshire terrier and all her furniture. She was ill and wanted to move to the city where her second husband had settled. It was a long trip; the truck broke down in the desert. But Nat King Cole's "Route 66" was on the radio when the beautiful San Francisco skyline appeared in front of us. What a moment! The singer seemed to share our triumph at reaching our destination.

A minister's son, Nathaniel Cole was born in Montgomery, Alabama, and grew up in Chicago. He started playing the piano at an early age, and in his teens formed a band with his brother. He settled on the West Coast, playing in clubs and bars and eventually on his own radio show, with a trio of piano, guitar, and bass that featured a beautifully blended sound. His smooth singing voice was just right for the ballads that became popular during World War II. "Straighten Up and Fly Right," his first hit record, was based on one of his father's sermons. It sold 500,000 copies.

On November 5, 1956, the *Nat King Cole Show* debuted on NBC, the first television show hosted by a black performer. Cole himself had said that he hoped to do for blacks on television what Jackie Robinson had done in sports. The show lasted slightly over a year, and its guests included Ella Fitzgerald and many other jazz and pop performers. But while it gained a large audience, sponsorship was always a problem, and finally the network canceled it. Nat King Cole was by then the top male jazz singer of his day and continued to perform steadily until his death from lung cancer.

SARAH VAUGHAN

Singer, pianist

1924 - 1991

I remember a day when my mother came home from one of her trips. My sister and I were very little, and we were playing in the backyard. My mother stepped around the corner of the house, smiling to see us. I knew from the look on her face that she loved me. Whenever I hear Sarah Vaughan sing "My Funny Valentine," I think of my mother and that smile.

Born in Newark, New Jersey, Sarah Vaughan always knew that she would be a musician. When she was sixteen, she sang "Body and Soul" at the legendary Amateur Night at Harlem's Apollo Theatre. She won the first prize of ten dollars and launched her career.

One of Sarah Vaughan's first engagements was with a band run by the pianist Earl "Fatha" Hines, which included Dizzy Gillespie and Charlie Parker. She has said that being in the band with the bebop players was just like being in school because she learned so much from them. She had a fine natural voice, and from the first could sing dazzling runs and glides. Like Billie Holiday and Ella Fitzgerald, Sarah Vaughan—often called "Sassy"—is one of the greatest singers to emerge from the jazz tradition.

INA SIMONE

Singer, pianist, composer

1933 -

In 1966, I was on board the U.S.S. *Constellation*, stationed off the coast of Vietnam. A friend from home sent me a Nina Simone tape. I played it over and over again; the anger and passion in her voice exactly matched my feeling that America was going crazy in Vietnam.

Born in Tryon, North Carolina, Simone exhibited virtuosity on the piano as a child and went on to study at the Juilliard School in New York City. Her first record album, *I Loves You, Porgy*, sold over a million copies. She soon found a voice in the black civil-rights movement with songs of protest like "Mississippi Goddamn." She has taken inspiration from the work of black poets like Paul Dunbar and Langston Hughes. One of her better-known songs is "Four Women," a stark portrait of the stereotypes assigned to black women in the United States.

In 1969, embittered by racism, Nina Simone renounced her homeland and moved to Europe, where she continues to perform and record. Her songs cross many musical boundaries—jazz, pop, blues, even rap—and have a strong poetic sense. She is one of the most original and versatile jazz musicians of the last three decades.

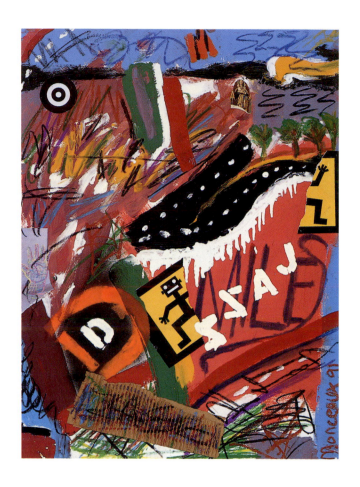

MILES DAVIS

Trumpeter, composer, bandleader

1926-1991

When I was eleven, my father gave me my own radio to keep in my bedroom. Each night, under my blanket, I'd tune in to Casey Kasem out of Atlanta. It was on his show that I first heard the haunting trumpet sounds of Miles Davis, who chased away the boogieman and helped me fall asleep.

Miles Davis was born into an Illinois family that, if not wealthy, was solidly middle-class. When he showed early musical promise, his father, a dentist, sent him to New York City's Juilliard School, the best-known music school in the country. But Davis quickly dropped out and was soon playing—and, for a time, living—with Charlie Parker. Davis made his name in bebop, but his style was less aggressive, more melodic and spare than Parker's and Gillespie's. This simplicity was a cornerstone of the cool jazz movement, which he helped to found. Like so many of the bebop players, Davis became involved with drugs during these years, but he was able to shake off the addiction.

Davis reinvented himself several times in his career. He was a breaker of rules, and because of that was always open to new ideas. In the 1970s, he incorporated elements of rock rhythm into his work. But he also brought a new emphasis on melody to jazz, with a gift for reducing a musical idea to its essence.

CHARLES MINGUS

String bass player, composer, bandleader, 1922-1979

54

In my freshman year at Bishop College, I was studying music intensively for the first time in my life. One day I received a box of Mingus's records from my sister. She had written on the box, "Let *this* be your music teacher. Love always, Elaine."

It's not easy to describe a Mingus sound. Where the Ellington band or a Lester Young solo is unmistakable, a Mingus bass line varies tremendously. And Mingus himself fought to avoid labels, to liberate the bass from its traditional subordinate role and to transcend what he felt were arbitrary limitations placed on jazz. Unlike most bass players, he didn't keep a steady rhythm, although the rhythm can be felt. Sometimes he literally slapped his bass or threw it around to get the effect he wanted. His music overflows with an emotional force that's just below the surface.

He was raised on church music during his childhood in Los Angeles. In school, he played first the trombone and then the cello. He switched to bass as a teenager, learning the swing tradition and eventually playing in a big band led by Louis Armstrong. But he also studied classical music. He was the only musician Duke Ellington ever fired – after a fight in which a trombonist pulled a knife on Mingus. The trombonist was an old problem, Ellington said, but Mingus seemed to have a whole new bag of tricks.

As a composer, Mingus came into his own in the 1950s. More than any other jazz composer, he expected his players to convey his emotional message, filtered through their own improvisations. His compositions were less structured, less likely to be written out than Ellington's. Their looser style inspired improvisation with great power. A passionate individualist in his life as well as his music, Mingus seemed to thrive on testing his musical limits and encouraging others to do so too.

My father didn't play a musical instrument, but he loved music. He was especially fond of the records of John Coltrane. On weekends when he didn't have to work, he'd hang around the house and play Coltrane's albums, not loud, but kind of quiet and for himself.

Coltrane is often looked on as a prophet in jazz, and sometimes it's hard to separate myth from fact. He grew up in North Carolina, and after a year in a musical conservatory and a stint in the navy, he began working as a clarinetist at the height of the bebop movement. After his switch to saxophone, his long apprenticeship included stints with Dizzy Gillespie, Miles Davis, and Thelonious Monk. Monk was especially influential, for both the eccentricity of his style and his high standards.

In the 1950s, drug and alcohol dependence, together with emotional difficulties, disrupted Coltrane's career. But in 1957, he broke his addictions – to drugs, alcohol, and cigarettes – in one week of fasting. At the same time, he embraced religion. And without the disruptive effect of the addictions, Coltrane's career gained new energy.

Coltrane's music generated great controversy in his day. On tenor and soprano saxophone, he would solo for fifteen minutes at a time, producing harsh, strange sounds that defied easy categorization. His music unnerved critics, including those who felt they were open to experimentation. He was heavily influenced by the music and religion of India, even naming his second son Ravi, after the great sitar player Ravi Shankar. He developed polytonality in jazz – the playing of a work in two keys at once, rather than one. In the 1960s, Coltrane moved into free jazz, which has no fixed meter or key. An obsessive, driven figure, he has inspired rock musicians as well as those working within the jazz tradition.

JOHN COLTRANE

Tenor and soprano saxophonist, composer, bandleader, 1926 - 1967

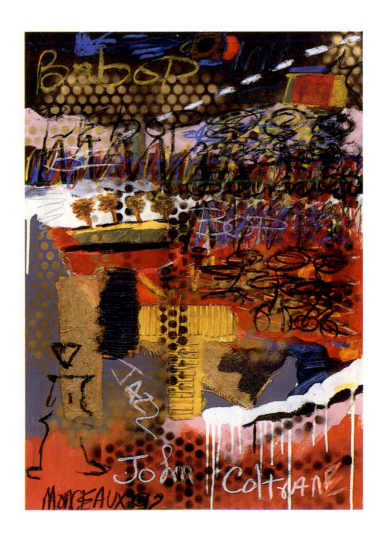

THE MODERN JAZZ QUARTET

John Lewis, pianist; Milt Jackson, vibraphonist; Percy Heath, bass player; Kenny Clarke, drummer; 1951-1974

My sister and I discovered the Modern Jazz Quartet when we were teenagers. We'd wandered into Fisher's music store on Lee Street in Alexandria, Virginia, and old Mr. Fisher had one of their records on the turntable. What a beautiful sound they had—it was crisp, like a crinoline petticoat. We left with three of their albums.

Founded in 1951 when four members of the Dizzy Gillespie band recorded an album, the Modern Jazz Quartet was one of the longest-lasting groups in jazz history. As John Lewis emerged as their leader, he showed himself to be a new kind of jazz composer. Nearly all jazz performance to date had featured an introductory chorus followed by a string of solos and a closing chorus. But Lewis was trained in classical music and brought an understanding of forms like the fugue and sonata to his work. He broke the mold, showing how a piece of music could build deliberately to a conclusion, and he was especially aware of how to shape the background sounds behind a soloist.

This didn't make the Modern Jazz Quartet sound classical, though. Milt Jackson was an improviser with strong roots in the blues tradition, and all four members of the quartet were schooled in bebop. But in general, their music is cooler and more in the classical tradition than most bebop. The Quartet's pieces evolved as the members continued to play and record them. When a work stopped suggesting directions for improvisation, they dropped it. Like many other players and groups in the 1960s and '70s, the Modern Jazz Quartet fused musical traditions in a quest for a style all their own.

JAZZ SINGERS ON THE STAGE

Pearl Bailey, 1918-1990

Lena Horne, 1917-

Starting with Josephine Baker, a few jazz singers have found stardom and a much wider audience on the stage. Pearl Bailey and Lena Horne are glamorous first ladies of jazz and the theater. Pearl Bailey started her career at the age of fifteen by winning an amateur contest. She sang and danced with various bands, and in 1946 made her Broadway debut with *Saint Louis Woman*. Her starring role in a Broadway production of *Hello, Dolly!* won her a Tony award. Lena Horne first appeared on stage at the age of six. In 1934, she dropped out of school to become a showgirl at the Cotton Club. She has sung with many bands and orchestras, and has had a successful film career. At the age of sixty-four, she starred in her own one-woman show, *Lena Horne: The Lady and Her Music*.

Johnetta

Singer

1927-1983

As children, my sister and I sometimes were taken to hear my mother sing in the clubs in New Orleans. She looked so beautiful up on stage. But my best memories are of when she was at home, going over new material. Sometimes we'd be outside and would look in the window to see her at the piano. Sometimes we'd sit on the piano bench next to her. She always told me, "Never forget the long, hard past history of your people. Your audiences will hear it in your music when you sing."

Johnetta played the piano as a child, but made a career as a singer in the after-hours world of New Orleans, California, and Europe. She has been linked with the leading blues women of the South. Starting in the 1940s, Johnetta began to work mostly as a soloist and gained widespread popularity with the rediscovery of the blues in the 1950s. She was known for the great warmth of her style, a rich soprano voice, and swinging melodies. She chose a life that required sacrifice and time apart from her family, which she regretted. But she was an inspiration.

GLOSSARY

arrangement the orchestration of a musical work – i.e., choosing which instruments play at what time, and where improvisation falls.

bebop a jazz style developed during the late 1930s and early 1940s, characterized by very fast tempos, complex melodies, and unusual chords. Bebop, which emphasized the inventiveness of soloists, was usually played in small groups.

blue note a note, usually the third, fifth, or seventh of a scale, that is flattened slightly rather than the pure scale tone. The blue note is derived from African music and is used often in jazz and the blues.

blues a secular folk music that rose among African Americans during the late 19th century and features several African influences: a call-and-response pattern, blue notes, and imitation of the human voice by musical instruments. Classic blues have a twelve-measure, three-line form, with the second line repeating the first.

boogie-woogie a style of piano developed in the late 1920s featuring hard-driving, repetitive figures played by the left hand and a freer right hand.

chord a combination of usually three or more notes sounded simultaneously or in succession.

cool jazz a jazz style that developed during the late 1940s and throughout the 1950s in reaction to bebop. Cool jazz has a clean, studied sound, complex textures, and a deliberate tone often with a slight lagging behind the beat.

creole a person born in Louisiana of French ancestry, often mixed with Negro stock. Black creoles were often of lighter skin and considered themselves to be of a higher social class than other blacks, and before the Civil War, they were more likely to be free citizens than slaves.

cutting contest (carving contest) a contest of skill between bands or individual musicians seeking to outplay, or "cut," each other.

gig a job, usually a paid one, to play music.

harmony the relation of the notes in a musical piece. The patterns formed by the notes create the key that the piece is in and, with rhythm, give it expressiveness and momentum.

improvisation music played without written notation, an instantaneous composition that is central to jazz.

jam session an informal gathering of musicians improvising and playing on their own time, usually after hours.

jive talk bantering, teasing talk, with many slang expressions, often associated with jazz musicians.

key the principal scale of a piece, in which many or most of its notes are played.

meter the basic succession of beats in a musical piece, the framework against which the rhythm is played.

pitch a note or musical tone.

race records starting in the 1920s, recordings made specifically for the African American market, usually specialty labels of major record companies.

ragtime an enormously popular musical style of the late 19th and early 20th century, consisting of a syncopated melody over a regularly accented beat.

riff a repeated brief musical phrase, used as background for a soloist or to add drama to a musical climax.

scat singing a singing style, usually improvised, that uses nonsense syllables for the words of a song, often with the goal of sounding like a musical instrument.

Storyville the red-light district in old New Orleans, where bordellos and music halls were concentrated, and where early jazz musicians were often hired to perform.

swing the commercial dance music associated with the 1930s and early '40s and played by the big bands; also, the element in jazz that defines it and separates it from classical music: a style of playing in which the rhythm is as important as the notes played, and in which the beats that are normally unaccented in classical music are given equal importance to the accented beats.

syncopation the shifting of a regular musical beat to place emphasis on a normally unaccented beat.

vodun, also voodoo a religion practiced at various times throughout the Caribbean and American South, incorporating aspects of Roman Catholicism and African religions, as well as African music, into its services.

INDEX